the Seven love letters of Jesus

A SMALL GROUP STUDY
PASTOR STEVE BERGER
WITH WAYNE HASTINGS

The Seven Love Letters of Jesus Study Guide
© 2009 by Steve Berger, Senior Pastor Grace Chapel

Printed in the United States

Cover and Interior design: Matt Dolan
Editor: Jennifer Hesse

ISBN 978-1-936355-01-3

CONTENTS

WELCOME

Studying God's word is a unique and special opportunity to hear His voice. It's my hope and prayer that as you read and reflect on these Scriptures your heart will be open to how God is guiding and leading you. Psalm 119:133 reads, "DIrect my steps by Your word, And let no iniquity have dominion over me." God's word guides. The Apostle Peter wrote, "Having been born again, not of corruptible seed but incorruptible, through the word of God which lives and abides forever." (1 Peter 1:23) God's word is alive and a source of new life. As you review this guide be prepared for God's word to show you new insights and sources of renewed faith life. Much thoughtful prayer, and study of God's word has gone into this book. It's a joy to know that you are using it as a part of your spiritual journey. You may also find the companion book to this study as a tool as you unpack the sessions and dive deeper into His word.

THE STUDY

Friends, in the next six chapters we are going to study seven letters the Lord Jesus lovingly wrote to seven churches located in seven cities in Asia (modern-day Turkey). These letters were preserved for us by the Apostle John in the Book of Revelation. John heard Jesus' words, and he wrote them not only to the seven churches but to us today. There is tremendous meaning and instruction for Christians today in these seven love letters. In the letter to the church at Pergamos, Jesus said: "He who has an ear, let him hear what the Spirit says to the churches. To him who overcomes I will give some of the hidden manna to eat" (Rev. 2:17).

TO HIM WHO OVERCOMES

Jesus wants us to overcome. He sees us in our self-propelled lives doing whatever to get along and missing the bigger picture that He's there for us. He wrote these seven letters to move us to become less dependent on everything but Him—and to do that, He encourages us to be overcomers.

Overcomers are not suddenly perfect people. Overcomers are not just okay with going to church and sitting nicely in the chairs, ready to shake somebody's hand or sing the next verse kind of people. Overcomers are people who know they have hurdles in their lives and know they need Jesus to get them over them. Overcomers are people, like you and me, who deeply desire to hear Jesus' voice and move away from the past. Overcomers choose to move on with their hand in Jesus' hand—one step at a time.

HIDDEN MANNA

In the desert during the Exodus, the Israelites were given the gift of manna. It fell from heaven and met every dietary need they had. After a while, however, they grew tired of the manna. They whined for other things—things that in the past never came close to satisfying them as the manna satisfied.

Friends, there are some tremendous lessons for us in these seven love letters. They are lessons directly from Jesus, and they are lessons that will meet every need we have. They are hard lessons, but they are the best lessons we can learn.

Don't get weary or tired as we move along. Trust God to help you see, with new eyes, some things about yourself and about your church that are distractions from totally trusting Him and knowing Him fully. Don't get tired of this precious manna, but enjoy it, even when it's hard.

· · · · · · · · · · · ·

▪ HOW TO USE THIS STUDY GUIDE

This study guide is for small group or personal use. Each session is broken into several parts.

First is an outline of the message or "message notes" from which this study guide was created. This outline should give you a good summary of the section of scripture that is being studied. As I mentioned above, more details of each session's message can be found in the accompanying book.

The second section is titled "Read and Reflect". In this section is more scripture for you to study and there are several questions for each passage to help you or your small group focus on what God is saying and how to apply it. Take your time as you go through this section. The point is to help you understand and apply God's word to your life. Moving quickly down the section and checking off the list of scriptures like a "to-do" list will only serve to get you through the scripture lessons as opposed to soaking them into your life and heart.

The third section is "Action Steps". This section is designed for you or your group to move from simply studying God's word to some kind of personal or group action. It may be more study and exhortations to pray or it may be some suggestions on some specific action steps you can take as a result of what you have just studied. Whatever the action step is, it's meant to bring the study alive in you and your group.

The final section is "Small Group Suggestions" and it is here to give the leaders of small groups and Sunday school classes some things to do within the group to enhance the study. They are guidelines that you can use to bring a richer experience to your group. Thank you for choosing this study and for jumping head first into God's word. I'm grateful to you for taking this step with me to learn how Jesus' love letters can bring His heart and message to us and for us.

With blessing and warm regards

Steve Berger
Pastor, Grace Chapel Church
Leipers Fork, TN

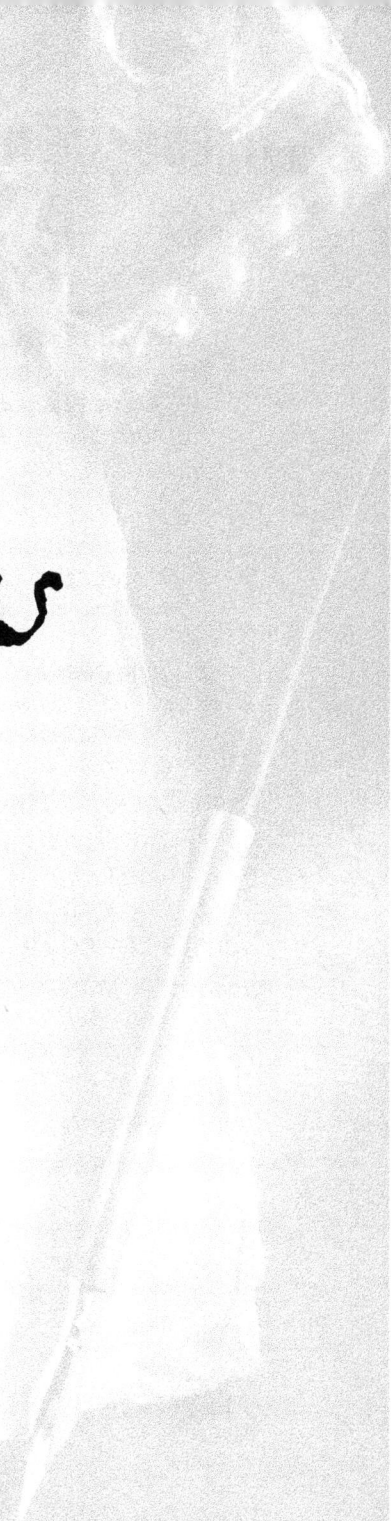

SESSION 1

Ephesus

■MESSAGE NOTES

1. Preface
    a. *We should be much more concerned today about the condition of the church and about what Jesus has to say to us in the Book of Revelation than we are about all the stuff that's up for grabs and interpretation.*
    b. *Jesus always challenges His church because He loves us, and when He sees us going just a bit astray, on whatever level, He loves us so much that He says, "Hey! I'm back over here. You went over there, but I'm back over here. Comeback, come back, come back."*

2. Background
    a. *The church was birthed at Pentecost, and sixty years have now passed.*
    b. *The apostle John is the only disciple left. He's an old guy, in his late eighties, maybe into his nineties, and he's exiled on the island of Patmos.*
    c. *John goes into the mouth of a cave and begins to worship. He sees something he's never seen before. It's called the Book of Revelation.*
    d. *The first letter in this section of Revelation is to the church at Ephesus, and that's what we're going to unpack.*

3. The Message: Revelation 2: 1-7
    a. *The church was sound in doctrine, active in service, and moral in conduct.*
    b. *However, the Ephesian Christians had lost their first love—Jesus.*

4. Christ's Loving Rebuke
    a. *You need to remember from where you've fallen.*
    b. *You need to remember that this problem can repeat itself.*
    c. *You need to remember to share your love.*

5. Christ's Simple Solution: *You need to repent.*

6. Christ's Simple Instruction: *You need to return.*
    a. *They were honest about their current level of experience with the Holy Spirit.*
    b. *They were teachable and responsive to further instruction.*
    c. *They were open and receptive to the Holy Spirit.*
    d. *They were magnifiers, worshipers of Jesus.*
    e. *They were transparent before each other.*

READ & REFLECT
REVELATION 2:1-7

¹ "To the angel of the church of Ephesus write, 'These things says He who holds the seven stars in His right hand, who walks in the midst of the seven golden lampstands:
² 'I know your works, your labor, your patience, and that you cannot bear those who are evil. And you have tested those who say they are apostles and are not, and have found them liars;
³ and you have persevered and have patience, and have labored for My name's sake and have not become weary.
⁴ Nevertheless I have this against you, that you have left your first love.
⁵ Remember therefore from where you have fallen; repent and do the first works, or else I will come to you quickly and remove your lampstand from its place—unless you repent.
⁶ But this you have, that you hate the deeds of the Nicolaitans, which I also hate.
⁷ He who has an ear,
let him hear what the Spirit says to the churches. To him who overcomes I will give to eat from the tree of life, which is in the midst of the Paradise of God.'"

· · · · · · · · · · · ·

1. *What good things did Jesus have to say to the church at Ephesus?*

2. *Why did He rebuke them?*

3. Describe the strengths and weaknesses of the Ephesian church.

4. What causes a person to lose their first love? Think back to when you first asked Christ into your life. How have things changed? What's caused the change?

5. Why does our love tend to grow cold? How do you bring back the special feelings of first love?

6. What do you need to change in your life so you can feel the power of loving Jesus for the first time?

[1] And it happened, while Apollos was at Corinth, that Paul, having passed through the upper regions, came to Ephesus. And finding some disciples

[2] he said to them, "Did you receive the Holy Spirit when you believed?" So they said to him, "We have not so much as heard whether there is a Holy Spirit."

[3] And he said to them, "Into what then were you baptized?" So they said, "Into John's baptism."

[4] Then Paul said, "John indeed baptized with a baptism of repentance, saying to the people that they should believe on Him who would come after him, that is, on Christ Jesus."

[5] When they heard this, they were baptized in the name of the Lord Jesus.

[6] And when Paul had laid hands on them, the Holy Spirit came upon them, and they spoke with tongues and prophesied.

[17] This became known both to all Jews and Greeks dwelling in Ephesus; and fear fell on them all, and the name of the Lord Jesus was magnified.

[18] And many who had believed came confessing and telling their deeds.

[19] Also, many of those who had practiced magic brought their books together and burned them in the sight of all. And they counted up the value of them, and it totaled fifty-thousand pieces of silver.

• • • • • • • • • • • •

1. What is your current experience with the Holy Spirit? Do you feel His power or doubt it? Why?

2. What does it mean to be teachable? How does a person learn to surrender his/her own opinion and learn something new?

3. Are you open and receptive to the Holy Spirit? Write or share a way you've seen the Holy Spirit work in your life.

4. How would you define true worship? What does this passage say about worshiping God? Do you expect to hear from God during worship, or do you look at your watch and hope the time will pass quickly?

5. How transparent are you? Do you have someone with whom you can share your feelings? Thoughts? Prayers? Dreams?

6. Take a moment and openly confess your heart to God.

■ ACTION STEPS

1. Take time each day to open your heart and mind to God's teaching and leading. Openly and regularly invite the Holy Spirit to come into your life—to guide, to teach, and to lead you to new understandings and deeper love for God.

2. Meditate on these two passages of Scripture. What do you personally need to do to become more honest about your experience with the Holy Spirit, teachable and responsive to further instruction from the Word, and open and receptive to the Holy Spirit?

3. What steps do you need to take to fully magnify and worship God with your life and become more transparent within the body of Christ?

4. Listen to worship music, and let God speak to you through it. What is He saying? What can you learn? Raise your hands in joy and gratefulness to Him and His promises to you. Open your heart to receive. Don't feel embarrassed—just rest in the power of the Holy Spirit through music and worship.

5. Actively read the Word of God, and listen for what God is saying to you personally through it. What can you learn? Pray back the Scriptures to God, and fill your heart with His promises. Open your heart to receive. Rest in His Word, speak it boldly even if you are alone, and feel the power of the Holy Spirt as you worship through the Word.

6. Pray. In your own words, ask God to fill you with the Holy Spirit, make you teachable and vulnerable, help you truly know how to worship Him, and help you identify and confess whatever might be holding you back from possessing the wonderful power.

■ SMALL GROUP SUGGESTIONS

- Start your time together with worship. Even if no one in your group can lead or sing, play worship music at the beginning (try a song like Open the Eyes of My Heart, Lord) and encourage the group to freely experience worship.

- As you run through the lesson, help the group look inward instead of outward to the church. Changing a church to be more like what Jesus described in these verses starts with the people being humble, open, and teachable. Seek to allow the Holy Spirit to use this lesson to change hearts of people, not to give an outlet for complaining or comparing churches.

- If your group is mostly comprised of married people, discuss how the metaphor of a couple's first love for one another relates to our first love for Christ. Why does the "first love" tend to grow cold? Ask members to share the things they did in the early days of their courtship. Ask people to share the things they did in the early days of their relationship with Christ. Do they feel a sense of loss?

- Be prepared for people to have questions about their current spiritual life. This could be a powerful session to lead some members of your group back to a loving, open relationship with Christ and the Holy Spirit. Don't be afraid of letting the group struggle with this. The power of the lesson is in opening hearts, not just getting through the lesson. As a leader, be patient, encouraging, and open to God's leading.

SESSION 2
Smyrna

■ MESSAGE NOTES

1. Preface
   a. *We are going to talk about suffering and what our response needs to be when we are suffering in and for Jesus.*
   b. *Smyrna was a wealthy city. It was known as the "Crown of Asia.*
   c. *Christians were under tremendous persecution in Smyrna.*

2. The Message: Revelation 2:8-11

3. You need to be eternally minded.
   a. *Don't look at pain; look at Me.*
   b. *Don't look at death; look at Me.*
   c. *Don't look at circumstances; look at Me.*

4. You need to know God as never before.
   a. *There are some realities of God, some of His truths that are only known in the place of crushing suffering.*
   b. *God's Word must be a reality in our hearts.*

5. You need to not be afraid of suffering.
   a. *Christians suffer because of ungodly behavior.*
   b. *Christians suffer to prevent pride.*
   c. *Christians suffer to learn trusting obedience.*
   d. *Christians suffer as a testimony of Jesus' preserving grace and power.*

6. You need to hear what the Spirit is saying: Be an overcomer!

READ & REFLECT
REVELATION 2:8-11

8 "And to the angel of the church in Smyrna write,'These things says the First and the Last, who was dead, and came to life:

9 'I know your works, tribulation, and poverty (but you are rich); and I know the blasphemy of those who say they are Jews and are not, but are a synagogue of Satan.

10 Do not fear any of those things which you are about to suffer. Indeed, the devil is about to throw some of you into prison, that you may be tested, and you will have tribulation ten days. Be faithful until death, and I will give you the crown of life.

11 He who has an ear, let him hear what the Spirit says to the churches. He who overcomes shall not be hurt by the second death.'"

· · · · · · · · · · · ·

1. Verse 8 describes Jesus as "the First and the Last," and verse 11 promises that those who overcome will "not be hurt by the second death." What is the link between these two verses and the challenges facing those in Smyrna? Facing you?

**2. Jesus says, "I know your poverty, but you are rich."
Describe in your own words what He means?**

.

**3. What are some of the things you could do today to be more
eternally minded?**

4. *When you face trials and problems, is your immediate response a plea for instant relief?*

5. *Review why Christians suffer. Think about when you have suffered. What has helped you feel free of the circumstances?*

6. *Define, in your own words, the "crown of life."*

7. *God told Joshua to be strong and courageous. What do you fear? How can God help you overcome that fear?*

READ JOB 1:20-22

20 Then Job arose, tore his robe, and shaved his head; and he fell to the ground and worshiped.

21 And he said: "Naked I came from my mother's womb, and naked shall I return there. The LORD gave, and the LORD has taken away; blessed be the name of the LORD."

22 In all this Job did not sin nor charge God with wrong.

. . . .

1. Why is Job's first response to worship?

2. How do you feel about your possessions? What if they were all taken from you? How do you think you would respond?

3. Have you ever been in a difficult circumstance and wondered why God would allow it to happen?

| **READ** 1 JOHN 4:4 |

You are of God, little children, and have overcome them, because He who is in you is greater than he who is in the world.

. . . .

1. Do you know someone who has overcome negative circumstances? How did they persevere?

2. What is the key to overcoming pain, suffering, and circumstances?

◼ ACTION STEPS

1. Reread Revelation 2:8–11. How does Smyrna compare to where you live? Are there people suffering and in need of Christ? How can you share your faith with them so they can become overcomers?

2. Take some time over the next few days to study Old Testament characters like Joshua, Caleb, Moses, Joseph, and Gideon. List the circumstances they met with in one column and then list how God helped them overcome. Make reference to the specific verse so the next time you experience trials you have a source of God's encouragement from His Word.

3. Develop a daily habit of reading Scripture, and then take time to listen for God's voice in His Word. Ask, "Spirit, what can I hear from You about what I've just read?" Listen.

SMALL GROUP SUGGESTIONS

- Start your time together with worship. Even if no one in your group can lead or sing, play worship music at the beginning (try a song like Open the Eyes of My Heart, Lord) and encourage the group to freely experience worship.

- This is a lesson on overcoming. Encourage your group to share their stories about how they have overcome circumstances, and help others who may be in the midst of it all to see God's power and love.

- Discuss openly the four reasons why Christians suffer. Be prepared for questions about how a loving God could cause pain and suffering. Point the group back to the teaching and Job's response to suffering. Read James 1:2 and let the group share about how they can count it all joy during difficult times.

- Stay focused on the passages of Scripture presented in the lesson. Bring your group to an understanding of the victory that Jesus has for them through their circumstances.

- Be prepared to listen and pray. People may share some things that require you to pray and support them. This is what small groups do best—support, love, and pray for each other.

SESSION 3

Pergamos and Thyatira

■ MESSAGE NOTES

1. Preface
    a. *We need to walk a tightrope between two sides of the spectrum: truth and love.*
    b. *Filter truth through God's Word alone.*
2. The Message: Revelation 2:12-29
3. Devilish Compromise
    a. *It's an abomination.*
    b. *It leads to death.*
    c. *It leads to a loss of inheritance.*
    d. *It leads to judgement and tribulation.*
4. Decide to Change
    a. *We must flee.*
    b. *We must take it seriously.*
5. There Is Hope
    a. *Repentance*
    b. *Eternal Satisfaction*
    c. *Pardon*
    d. *Real Intimacy*
    e. *Himself*

READ & REFLECT
REVELATION 2:12-29

^{12} "And to the angel of the church in Pergamos write, 'These things says He who has the sharp two-edged sword:

^{13} "I know your works, and where you dwell, where Satan's throne is. And you hold fast to My name, and did not deny My faith even in the days in which Antipas was My faithful martyr, who was killed among you, where Satan dwells.

^{14} But I have a few things against you, because you have there those who hold the doctrine of Balaam, who taught Balak to put a stumbling block before the children of Israel, to eat things sacrificed to idols, and to commit sexual immorality.

^{15} Thus you also have those who hold the doctrine of the Nicolaitans, which thing I hate.

^{16} Repent, or else I will come to you quickly and will fight against them with the sword of My mouth.

^{17} He who has an ear, let him hear what the Spirit says to the churches. To him who overcomes I will give some of the hidden manna to eat. And I will give him a white stone, and on the stone a new name written which no one knows except him who receives it.'"

^{18} "And to the angel of the church in Thyatira write, These things says the Son of God, who has eyes like a flame of fire, and His feet like fine brass:

^{19} "I know your works, love, service, faith, and your patience; and as for your works, the last are more than the first.

^{20} Nevertheless I have a few things against you, because you allow that woman Jezebel, who calls herself a prophetess, to teach and seduce My servants to commit sexual immorality and eat things sacrificed to idols.

21 And I gave her time to repent of her sexual immorality, and she did not repent.

22 Indeed I will cast her into a sickbed, and those who commit adultery with her into great tribulation, unless they repent of their deeds.

23 I will kill her children with death, and all the churches shall know that I am He who searches the minds and hearts. And I will give to each one of you according to your works.

24 Now to you I say, and to the rest in Thyatira, as many as do not have this doctrine, who have not known the depths of Satan, as they say, I will put on you no other burden.

25 But hold fast what you have till I come.

26 And he who overcomes, and keeps My works until the end, to him I will give power over the nations—

27 'He shall rule them with a rod of iron; they shall be dashed to pieces like the potter's vessels'—as I also have received from My Father;

28 and I will give him the morning star.

29 He who has an ear, let him hear what the Spirit says to the churches.'"

• • • • • • • • • • • •

1. What does the word compromise mean to you? When is it acceptable to compromise? When isn't it acceptable?

2. Why is gaining social acceptance so important to us? What are some ways to make sure we're living by God's Word instead of tolerating the ways of the world?

3. The church at Pergamos did some good things—what were they? What does itmean, in your own words, to be loyal to Jesus?

4. The message to Thyatira sets limits on tolerance (v. 20). Describe some of the limits you have set for yourself based on what you read in Scripture.

5. *Reread verse 25. What is Jesus referring to when He says, "Hold fast what you have till I come"? To what would He expect us to hold tightly?*

6. *What does Jesus offer us in verses 26–28?*

7. What does Jesus mean when He says, "And he who overcomes and keeps My works until the end, to him I will give power over the nations"?

READ 1 CORINTHIANS 10:18–22

¹⁸ Observe Israel after the flesh: Are not those who eat of the sacrifices partakers of the altar?

¹⁹ What am I saying then? That an idol is anything, or what is offered to idols is anything?

²⁰ Rather, that the things which the Gentiles sacrifice they sacrifice to demons and not to God, and I do not want you to have fellowship with demons.

²¹ You cannot drink the cup of the Lord and the cup of demons; you cannot partake of the Lord's table and of the table of demons.

²² Or do we provoke the Lord to jealousy? Are we stronger than He?

• • • • • • • • • • • •

1. What is the best way for us not to be deceived?

2. Who is our hope (v. 11)?

3. What does it mean to be washed? Sanctified? Justified?

■ ACTION STEPS

1. First Kings 16—22 chronicles the story of Jezebel. Take some time to read about her and all she did to turn the eyes of Israel away from God. Reflect on things that happen in our day and age that take our eyes away from God and His teaching. How can you safeguard yourself, your family, and your church from modern-day Jezebels?

2. The good news is that it's not too late for us. Jesus stands waiting for us to repent. He wants to give us all we need. Whatever it is you've done, He's there waiting for you. Why don't you ask Him right now to forgive you, to satisfy every desire, to welcome you into His arms, and to begin that intimacy only Jesus can give?

■ SMALL GROUP SUGGESTIONS

- Start your time together with worship and prayer. Develop a list of some specific issues (based on this lesson) that are affecting us today, and pray specifically for them.

- This is a lesson on hope. Encourage your group to share their stories about hope and repentance.

- Openly discuss the issues and be prepared to lead the group through some hard teaching. Prepare yourself through the scriptures mentioned in the teaching. It's important that you lead and facilitate, not argue or threaten. Let Scripture teach and give hope.

- Go deeper into the scriptures provided in the lesson. Read each one aloud and then talk about them. What lessons come from the scriptures? What is God telling us?

- Be sure to give time at the end for prayer and perhaps even open confession. This should be a time for support and loving hope as people come to realize and speak about compromise and immorality in their lives. Keep in mind, and help people realize, that Christ offers hope through repentance, eternal satisfaction, pardon, real intimacy, and Himself.

SESSION 4
Sardis

■ MESSAGE NOTES

1. Preface
   - *a. We have studied four letters:*
     - *i. Ephesus the loveless church*
     - *ii. Smyrna the persecuted church*
     - *iii. Pergamos and Thyatira the compromising churches*
   - *b. New letter to Sardis and Jesus has few good things to say to them*
   - *c. Rememer, He loves us too much to leave us like we are*

2. Background
   - *a. Sardis was an extremely wealthy and secure city.*
   - *b. The believers in Sardis were complacent. They comforted themselves right into death.*

3. The Message: Revelation 3:1–6

4. Jesus' Title: The Seven Spirits of God

5. Sardis' Condition: Dead and Resting

6. Sardis' Results: Incomplete Works

7. Jesus' Warning
   - *a. I am going to come when you least expect it.*
   - *b. Stop living this way.*

10. Jesus' Solution
   - *a. Wake Up*
   - *b. Strengthen What Remains*
   - *c. Hold Fast*
   - *d. Turn Back*

11. Jesus' Hope
   - *a. You can overcome spiritual death.*
   - *b. I will walk with you.*

READ & REFLECT
REVELATION 3:1-6

[1] "To the angel of the church in Sardis write, 'These things says He who has the seven Spirits of God and the seven stars: "I know your works, that you have a name that you are alive, but you are dead.

[2] Be watchful, and strengthen the things which remain, that are ready to die, for I have not found your works perfect before God.

[3] Remember therefore how you have received and heard; hold fast and repent. Therefore if you will not watch, I will come upon you like a thief, and you will not know what hour I will come upon you.

[4] You have a few names even in Sardis who have not defiled their garments; and they shall walk with Me in white, for they are worthy.

[5] He who overcomes shall be clothed in white garments, and I will not blot out his name from the Book of Life, but I will confess his name before my Father and before His angels.

[6] He who has an ear, let him hear what the Spirit says to the churches."'"

. . . .

1. How does Sardis compare to your city? Is your city wealthy? Is it poor?

2. How does comfort lead to complacency?

3. Have you ever attended a dead church? What was it like? What characteristics made it dead?

4. What do you think Jesus means when He points out that the works of the people in Sardis are not complete? Is your faith a destination or a long journey? Explain.

5. What are some things a complacent person can do to start again? What are some first steps? What is holding you back from starting?

6. Why was it important for Jesus to warn the people in Sardis that they would not know what time He was coming?

2 The Spirit of the LORD shall rest upon Him, the Spirit of wisdom and understanding, the Spiritof counsel and might, the Spirit of knowledge and of the fear of the LORD.

• • • • • • • • • • • •

1. Define, in your own words, what it means for the Spirit of the Lord to rest on you.

2. What is the "Spirit of wisdom"? What is the difference between wisdom and understanding? How can you gain more wisdom? How can you gain more understanding?

3. The "Spirit of counsel" refers to the ability to adopt right conclusions. How can you do this?

4. Living in the power or might of the Spirit means carrying out those right conclusions. What do you need to do so that you are living with the Spirit of the Lord resting on you, making good decisions and carrying them out? 5. Describe the fear of 5. Describe the fear of the Lord. What does it mean to you?

■ ACTION STEPS

1. Study Exodus 32:30–35. The people of Israel were complacent; they moved away from worshiping God to worshiping idols. What can you learn from this about remaining in the power of the Spirit and about how complacency and sin offend God?

2. Just as we discussed in the last chapter, the good news is that it's not too late for us. Jesus stands waiting for us to wake up, watch out, hold fast, and repent. Take a few minutes to pray and ask God to show you where you have become comfortable in your faith. What are areas that need to be awakened? Tell Him right now in prayer.

■ SMALL GROUP SUGGESTIONS

- Start your time together with worship and prayer. Specifically pray for your church and other churches to be on fire for God's Word and His plan.

- This lesson should strike a familiar note. Most of us in this world are very comfortable. We have plenty and, in many ways, we're a lot like the church in Sardis. Discuss any similarities you see. What do these similarities show us?

- Discuss what your group might do to be more involved with a local need. Choose a ministry from your church, or in your community that you could help. Consider ways that directly meet the ministries' needs.

- Discuss how we can be overcomers. What do we see in our current culture that causes us to need to wake up? How can we overcome the wealth and the complacency it can bring?

- Think about the command "hold fast." What does that mean? How can it be achieved in the group and in the church? (Consider accountability and prayer.)

- Allow time at the end of the session for prayer and confession. Like the last lesson, this is not a time to judge, but to love and pray.

SESSION 5

Philadelphia

■MESSAGE NOTES

1. Preface
   a. *This letter has some very encouraging words*
   b. *A fresh vision of what it means to be a passionate and equipped servant of Jesus Christ*
   c. *End result of this chapter: "I want what is said about them to be said about me."*

2. Background: A Young Outpost City
   a. *Sardis was an extremely wealthy and secure city.*
   b. *The believers in Sardis were complacent. They comforted themselves right into death.*

3. The Message: Revelation 3:7-13

4. The Authority
   a. *Jesus has the key of David.*
   b. *He can open the door to kingdom resources.*

5. The Opening
   a. *Open Door Observations*
      i. *Jesus is the One who opens kingdom doors.*
      ii. *Jesus is the One who keeps kingdom doors open.*
      iii. *We must recognize open doors.*
      iv. *We must pray for open doors.*
   b. *Why Jesus Chose Philadelphia*
      i. *They had little strength in themselves.*
      ii. *They kept His Word.*
      iii. *They didn't deny His name.*
   c. *Faithfulness in Small Beginnings*

6. The Promise
   a. *They had already passed the test.*
   b. *They would be saved from the worldwide trial.*

7. The Exhortation
   a. *Jesus is coming quickly.*
   b. *Hold fast; don't let anyone take your crown or your song.*

8. The Reward
   a. *Overcomers will be secure and immovable in the presence of God.*
   b. *Overcomers will be marked as God's own adopted children and servants.*

READ & REFLECT
REVELATION 3:7-13

[7] "And to the angel of the church in Philadelphia write,'These things says He who is holy, He who is true, "He who has the key of David, He who opens and no one shuts, and shuts and no one opens":

[8] "I know your works. See, I have set before you an open door, and no one can shut it; for you have a little strength, have kept My word, and have not denied My name.

[9] Indeed I will make those of the synagogue of Satan, who say they are Jews and are not, but lie—indeed I will make them come and worship before your feet, and to know that I have loved you.

[10] Because you have kept My command to persevere, I also will keep you from the hour of trial which shall come upon the whole world, to test those who dwell on the earth.

[11] Behold, I am coming quickly! Hold fast what you have, that no one may take your crown.

[12] He who overcomes, I will make him a pillar in the temple of My God, and he shall go out no more. I will write on him the name of My God and the name of the city of My God, the New Jerusalem, which comes down out of heaven from My God. And I will write on him My new name.

[13] He who has an ear, let him hear what the Spirit says to the churches.""

• • • • • • • • • • •

1. What comes to mind when you think of an outpost city? What would it have been like to be a citizen in such an environment?

2. Think back to a time when you walked through an open door from Jesus. What characterized it? How did you recognize it as an open door from Jesus? How did you feel? What was the ultimate result?

3. What were the three reasons Jesus had for opening a door for the Philadelphians? Define what each means in your own words. Search the Scriptures for passages that will help you hold firm to the three reasons.

4. What was Jesus' promise to the Philadelphians? Why? What do you think needs to be done to pass the test?

5. Write out Jesus' exhortation to them. How does it apply to you today?

6. What is the ultimate reward? Define a life focused on achieving the ultimate reward that Jesus promises in this passage.

10 Now there was a certain disciple at Damascus named Ananias; and to him the Lord said in a vision, "Ananias." And he said, "Here I am, Lord."

11 So the Lord said to him, "Arise and go to the street called Straight, and inquire at the house of Judas for one called Saul of Tarsus, for behold, he is praying.

12 And in a vision he has seen a man named Ananias coming in and putting his hand on him, so that he might receive his sight."

13 Then Ananias answered, "Lord, I have heard from many about this man, how much harm he has done to your saints in Jerusalem.

14 And here he has authority from the chief priests to bind all who call on Your name."

15 But the Lord said to him, "Go, for he is a chosen vessel of Mine to bear My name before Gentiles, kings, and the children of Israel. 16 For I will show him how many things he must suffer for My name's sake."

17 And Ananias went his way and entered the house; and laying his hands on him he said, "Brother Saul, the Lord Jesus, who appeared to you on the road as you came, has sent me that you may receive your sight and be filled with the Holy Spirit."

18 Immediately there fell from his eyes something like scales, and he received his sight at once; and he arose and was baptized.

• • • • • • • • • • •

1. What was Ananias's first response to the Lord's voice?

2. Read 1 Samuel 3:1–10. What was Samuel's response to the Lord's calling and the open door?

3. How did Ananias "sift through" the message? How can we be wise stewards and discern possible false doors?

4. How long did Ananias wait after God told him to go? What would waiting have meant?

5. What did Ananias's response mean to Saul?

6. What about Ananias's character and spiritual life led Jesus to choose him for this open door?

■ ACTION STEPS

1. Study Exodus 3:1—4:17.
   a. *What was Moses' initial response to the Lord's voice in verse 5?*
   b. *Make a list of Moses' five objections and the Lord's five answers seen in Exodus 3:11–4:17. Which of Moses' objections do you identify with most? Take a moment to ponder the sufficiency of the Lord's responses.*
   c. *Read Exodus 5:1, Deuteronomy 34:10–12, and 1 Samuel 12:6 How did Moses change? What did God accomplish through him?*
   d. *Spend time in prayer responding to this study. Express to God your willingness to be changed and used by Him for His purposes.*

2. Ask God to help you see His open door opportunities for you.

3. Seek His wisdom to overcome the tendency to trust your own strength. Seek His strength to not shrink back from God-given opportunities.

4. Commit to knowing and defending His Word and to fully accepting His will for your life.

■ SMALL GROUP SUGGESTIONS

• Start your time together with worship and prayer. Specifically pray that your group and your church will be ready when God opens doors.

• This lesson could encourage your group to take action. Your church, your community, and your group may see many open doors for service. Sift through the opportunities and walk through the doors as a group. It will help you build a stronger, more focused small group.

• Continue your discussion from previous lessons about how to be overcomers. What made the church at Philadelphia unique? Why were they chosen? Which of their qualities or behaviors do you think prompted Jesus to give them so much?

- Allow people to share their stories about walking through God-given doors. What made an opportunity unique? What can the group learn from those experiences? Ask someone to share about opportunities that were in his or her own strength instead of God-led. What can you learn from those stories?

- Allow time at the end of the session for prayer. This can be a time of celebration as God leads you to new opportunities to serve and honor Him.

SESSION 6

Laodicea

◼ MESSAGE NOTES

1. Preface
   a. *We've come to the conclusion, after studying six letters, that when Jesus challenges or corrects His church, it's never for the purpose of just rubbing their noses in their failure.*
   b. *We're studying these letters so we could see our need for change and then respond to Jesus' hope and health for us.*
   c. *The church in this session, the church in Laodicea, most reflects the church in the Western world today.*

2. Background
   a. *A Wealthy Inland City*
   b. *Phrygian Eye Salve*
   c. *Black Wool*

3. Early Concerns
   a. *Paul's Concerns*
   b. *Epaphras's Concerns*

4. The Message: Revelation 3:14–22

5. Who's in Charge?
   a. *The Laodiceans believed their church was their own.*
   b. *Anytime a church becomes a church of the people, it's in trouble.*

6. His Dismantling
   a. *Sometimes lives have to be dismantled before they can be built up.*
   b. *The Laodiceans' spiritual condition was like their aqueduct's lukewarm water.*
   c. *Jesus gave them tough love.*

7. His Indictment
   a. *They saw themselves drastically differently than the way Jesus saw them.*
   b. *They were in spiritual slumber.*

8. His Counsel
   a. *They should submit to Jesus refining work in their lives.*
   b. *They should be clothed in Jesus white garments of holiness and righteousness.*
   c. *They should see their true spiritual condition through the Word of God.*

9. His Hope
   a. *Jesus rebuked them because He loved them, and He wasn't willing to let them stay where they were.*
   b. *They should be zealous and repent.*

10. His Knock
    a. *He was near them but still outside the door.*
    b. *He called them to open it.*

11. His Promise
    a. *People cannot keep being in charge of their lives and call Jesus Lord at the same time.*
    b. *The Laodiceans could sit on Jesus' throne with Him if they gave up sitting on their own thrones of wealth and self-satisfaction.*

READ & REFLECT
REVELATION 3:14-22

---

14 "And to the angel of the church of the Laodiceans write, 'These things says the Amen, the Faithful and True Witness, the Beginning of the creation of God:

15 "I know your works, that you are neither cold nor hot. I could wish you were cold or hot.

16 So then, because you are lukewarm, and neither cold nor hot, I will vomit you out of My mouth.

17 Because you say, 'I am rich, have become wealthy, and have need of nothing'—and do not know that you are wretched, miserable, poor, blind, and naked—

18 I counsel you to buy from Me gold refined in the fire, that you may be rich; and white garments, that you may be clothed, that the shame of your nakedness may not be revealed; and anoint your eyes with eye salve, that you may see.

19 As many as I love, I rebuke and chasten. Therefore be zealous and repent.

20 Behold, I stand at the door and knock. If anyone hears My voice and opens the door, I will come in to him and dine with him, and he with Me.

²¹ To him who overcomes I will grant to sit with Me on My throne, as I also overcame and sat down with My Father on His throne.

²² "He who has an ear, let him hear what the Spirit says to the churches." ' "

* * * * * * * * * * * *

1. What parallels do you see between the city of Laodicea and a modern Western city?

2. Jesus referred to Himself as "the Amen, the Faithful and the True Witness," which means that He is the very foundation of faithfulness and truth. Why do you think it was important for Him to begin the letter with that declaration?

3. *Jesus talked about water, gold, and garments. Why was it important for Him to speak of things they understood? What are the things that are important to people today? How would Jesus contrast Himself to those things?*

4. *Describe in your own words what it means to have a lukewarm spiritual life.*

5. Jesus was not scolding this church; He was fighting with them. He was throwing water on them out of love so they would repent and return to Him. Describe the love Jesus had for the church of Laodicea, for your church, and for you.

6. What do you think it would be like to sit with Jesus on His throne? To sit with God on His throne?

7. What does it mean to you that Jesus also overcame?

READ COL. 2:1-2; 4:12-13, 16

¹ For I want you to know what a great conflict I have for you and those in Laodicea, and for as many as have not seen my face in the flesh,

² that their hearts may be encouraged, being knit together in love, and attaining to all riches of the full assurance of understanding, to the knowledge of the mystery of God, both of the Father and of Christ

¹² Epaphras, who is one of you, a bondservant of Christ, greets you, always laboring fervently for you in prayers, that you may stand perfect and complete in all the will of God.

¹³ For I bear him witness that he has a great zeal for you, and those who are in Laodicea, and those in Hierapolis

¹⁶ Now when this epistle is read among you, see that it is read also in the church of the Laodiceans, and that you likewise read the epistle from Laodicea.

● ● ● ● ● ● ● ● ● ● ● ●

1. *Why do you think Paul and Epaphras had concerns thirty years before the letter from Jesus was written in the Book of Revelation?*

2. *How would you describe Paul and Epaphras's attitude toward and responses to the warning signs they saw in the Laodiceans?*

3. How did the Laodiceans seem to respond to Paul and Epaphras's concerns and challenges?

4. When you receive loving correction, how do you respond? Do you hope to change the way you respond?

⁸ And Ephraim said,

'Surely I have become rich,

I have found wealth for myself;

In all my labors They shall find in me

no iniquity that is sin.'

. . . .

1. The people of Ephraim boasted in riches. How does this attitude mirror the people of Laodicea? The Western church?

2. Notice how many times the verse above mentions "me" or "myself." What does that tell you about the people of Ephraim? Could they have been truly reliant on God for everything?

3. How does God view our wealth? Our status? All our labors?

4. Reread Ephraim's boast at the end. Is completely trusting in yourself for everything a sin?

■ ACTION STEPS

1. Ask God to help you see your own lukewarmness and tendency to trust your own plan over God's plan. Offer your willingness to re spond to His loving correction with humility and obedience, to em brace His will, and to live for Him zealously.

2. The church at Laodicea was guided by people instead of the Lord. What is guiding your life? Your church? Pray for more or continued submission to God's leading in your life and church.

3. Jesus was willing to have the Laodiceans return to Him. What does that mean to you?

4. Pray for anyone you are aware of who needs to return to Jesus or come to Him for the first time. Ask God to speak to their hearts, lead them to repentance, and draw them into an intimate relationship with Himself.

■ SMALL GROUP SUGGESTIONS

- Start your time together with worship and prayer.

- This lesson should encourage your group to do some introspective thinking. Be prepared to talk about life's priorities and the battle of trusting self versus trusting Jesus.

- This is the concluding session. It would be a good idea to go through a review of all seven letters with the group.

- Allow people to share their stories about how they have reprioritized their lives. Ask people to share about a time when God was not at the center of their lives. Encourage an attitude of thankfulness and prayer so people will clearly know how much they are loved by Jesus and by the group for coming back to Christ.

- Allow time at the end of the session for prayer. This can be a time of celebration as you wrap up this lesson and summarize what the group has learned and is ready to change based on the teaching of these scriptures.